PACIFIC COAST MAMMAL FINDER

Identifying Pacific Coast Mammals by Their Tracks, Skulls, and Other Signs

RON RUSSO

illustrated by PAM FRAZIER

Nature Study
Guild Publish[...]

an imprint of Adventure[...]

T0275185

HOW TO USE THIS BOOK

If you've seen a mammal, go to pages 8 and 9. If you've found:

- prints or tracks, go to page 12.
- a skull or jawbone, go to pages 5–7.
- droppings, go to pages 10 and 11.
- nests, depressions, burrows, or mounds, go to pages 13 and 14.
- chew, scratch or browse marks, or other signs, go to pages 15–17.

CAUTION: WILDLIFE VIEWING

All animals in the outdoors are **wild,** even those in national and state parks. People should never approach any wild animal, no matter how docile it may appear. Each year, visitors die from approaching elk, moose, bison, and bears too closely. *If you need a close-up photo, get the proper camera and lens.*

Key features

On some illustrations, lines point out traits that are important to identification.

Seasons

Breeding seasons or other periods stated in the text represent normal periods, which can be offset by inclement weather, poor health and nutrition, disease, and other factors.

Dimensions

Unless otherwise indicated, dimensions given here are for length. Track illustrations represent prints left by a walking animal. Measurements next to each print are for the whole hind foot, which is longer than the print.

© 2024 Ron Russo (text), Pam Frazier (illustrations); © 1987 Nature Study Guild • ISBN 978-0-912550-38-1 • Printed in China • Cataloging-in-Publication data is available from the Library of Congress • naturestudy.com

MAMMAL ECOLOGY

Mammals in the wild are elusive. When you are hiking in the outdoors, they are likely to see, hear, or smell you first. If you do see a mammal, pages 8–9 will help identify it. You are more likely, however, to find one of the signs that indicates their presence. Often footprints (see page 12); droppings (see pages 10 and 11); skulls or jaws (see pages 5–7); or burrows, nests, and scratch or chew marks (see pages 13–17) will be the only things you will find to prove that mammals are around.

Mammals are different from other organisms because they have fur, large brains, a highly refined sense of hearing, and a variety of skin glands. Mammals also suckle their young and spend an extended time caring for them.

Body temperature

Mammals keep warm under a coat of hair or fur. To protect against winter temperatures, many mammals develop thicker, longer fur. This extra fur is shed in the spring with the onslaught of warmer weather. Deer get extra insulation from the trapped air inside their hollow hairs. Mammals can control body temperature (so that it stays fairly constant) by panting, sweating, and confining activity to the cooler hours. Not all mammals have the same body temperature. It generally varies quite a bit among different groups of mammals.

Mammals living in desert regions must confine their activity to the cooler nights when the chances of overheating and losing precious body water are much lower.

Some mammals found in the Pacific Coast states are beyond the scope of a small book and are not included here: shrews, kangaroo rats, mice, old-world rats, marine mammals, domestic mammals, and humans.

Many desert mammals get all the water they need from the food they eat. They control sweating, and concentrate their urine and droppings, retaining as much water as possible. Kangaroo rats have gone a step further with developed nasal traps that remove moisture from their exhaling breath.

Mammals, in any environment, that are active by night and quiet by day are called **nocturnal.** Sometimes you can spot nocturnal mammals by the shine reflected from eyes specially equipped for night vision when struck by the light of a car or campfire.

Camouflage

The color of mammal hair generally blends with the terrain, which helps them avoid detection by prey or predators. Many mammals, like hares and rabbits, remain motionless when approached by a predator. They rely on their camouflage and motionless form until the predator gets too close. At this point, the only escape is a speedy getaway. Quail and pheasants also use this tactic. Most mammals do not see color but only shades of black and white. A still, well-concealed animal may never be seen by a predator, even though it may pass within a few feet. In some mammals, like squirrels, all-black (melanistic) individuals are occasionally seen.

Reproduction

Mammals have one of the most successful forms of reproduction in the animal kingdom. The development of the young within a placental sac provides nourishment directly from the mother, along with protection from bacteria. The survival rate of fetuses tends to be high, as is the survival of newborns because of extended post-birth care. Although many are born naked and blind, others are ready to go. Antelope fawns are able to stand and run within a few minutes after birth.

Antlers and horns

Some mammals have antlers or horns growing from their skulls. Male members of the deer family—and both sexes of caribou—produce antlers. Antlers grow externally from calcium deposited by blood-filled capillaries underneath furred skin. By late summer, growth stops and the furry skin, called **velvet**, is rubbed off against tree trunks and small saplings (see key, page 15). Antlers are sharpened for use and display during the fall mating season. They are shed in winter, with regrowth starting in the spring.

In contrast, horns grow from an inner core of calcium-rich blood tissue. Antelope horns are shed annually, but those of bighorn sheep are permanent and grow to spectacular sizes and shapes. Males competing for females judge each others' status by the size and shape of horns, antlers, and physique. Both pronghorn antelope and bighorn sheep females have smaller horns than males.

Evergrowing teeth

Rabbits and rodents have incisors that grow continuously, an adaptation to grit in their diet that would otherwise wear their teeth to the gumline. If these animals don't have enough grit in their food, or are unable to gnaw regularly, their incisors will grow outside of their skulls and protrude from their mouths. If unchecked, these teeth will continue to grow until they turn backwards toward the skull, preventing the animal from eating. Starvation and death result.

Territories

Mammals often restrict their activities to a definite area called a **home range.** In order to get enough to eat, attract mates, and survive, mammals often defend all or a part of their home range as their **territory.** A defended territory usually has enough food, shelter, and nesting material to support a male and female of the same species. Nonbreeding animals usually exist in unclaimed zones or strips found between two or more territories of their species. Territory owners usually patrol their boundaries, marking them in prescribed locations with scent, urine, or droppings. Intruders of the same species are routinely driven off. The size of territories varies from year to year as the availability of food and other essential resources changes. If food is plentiful, territories are smaller than the previous year. Territories expand in response to scarcity. The territories of different, noncompeting species usually overlap.

Parasites

Wild mammals support a wide variety of hitchhiking parasites like fleas, ticks, blood-sucking flies, and lice. Parasites can weaken their hosts but rarely kill them. Because some of these parasites can transmit diseases like Lyme disease, plague, and tularemia to people, it is a good idea to **avoid handling dead animals,** especially rodents and rabbits.

Skin glands

Mammals have five different kinds of skin glands, which serve specific purposes.

Mammary glands in females produce milk to nurse young. Sweat glands help to cool mammals and get rid of waste products through the pores of the skin. Oil glands lubricate skin and hair. Scent and musk glands produce chemicals used for marking territories and communication.

Careful observation, curiosity, and this guidebook will help you enjoy the mammals of the Pacific Coast states.

SKULLS

Dental formulas

The dental formula for a skull or jaw is made by noting the numbers of each kind of tooth, from the front center to the rear of one side. Separate counts are made for the teeth attached to the skull and those in the jaw bone.

A formula of:

$$\frac{1\ 0\ 1\ 3}{1\ 0\ 1\ 3}$$

indicates that one incisor, no canine, one premolar, and three molars should normally be present on each side of both the skull and the jawbone. This formula matches the squirrel teeth illustrated to the right.

Health and age may cause teeth to be missing. So, a specimen you find may not precisely match the stated formula.

If you find a skull or jawbone, try to match it with the ones on the next pages. The dental formula will appear on the page indicated.

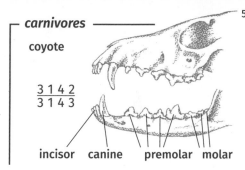

carnivores

coyote

$$\frac{3\ 1\ 4\ 2}{3\ 1\ 4\ 3}$$

incisor   canine   premolar molar

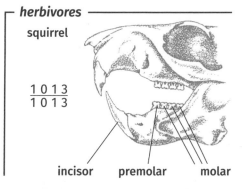

herbivores

squirrel

$$\frac{1\ 0\ 1\ 3}{1\ 0\ 1\ 3}$$

incisor   premolar   molar

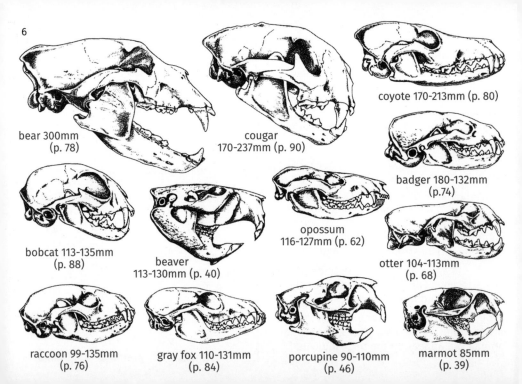

6

bear 300mm
(p. 78)

cougar
170-237mm (p. 90)

coyote 170-213mm (p. 80)

badger 180-132mm
(p.74)

bobcat 113-135mm
(p. 88)

beaver
113-130mm (p. 40)

opossum
116-127mm (p. 62)

otter 104-113mm
(p. 68)

raccoon 99-135mm
(p. 76)

gray fox 110-131mm
(p. 84)

porcupine 90-110mm
(p. 46)

marmot 85mm
(p. 39)

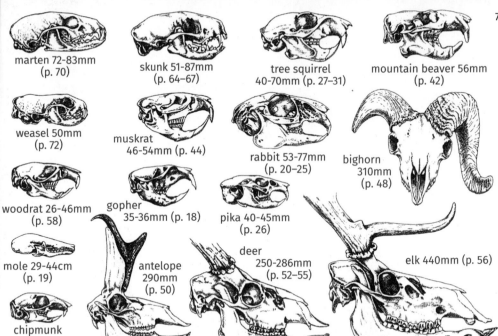

7

marten 72-83mm
(p. 70)

skunk 51-87mm
(p. 64–67)

tree squirrel
40-70mm (p. 27–31)

mountain beaver 56mm
(p. 42)

weasel 50mm
(p. 72)

muskrat
46-54mm (p. 44)

rabbit 53-77mm
(p. 20–25)

bighorn
310mm
(p. 48)

woodrat 26-46mm
(p. 58)

gopher
35-36mm (p. 18)

pika 40-45mm
(p. 26)

mole 29-44cm
(p. 19)

antelope
290mm
(p. 50)

deer
250-286mm
(p. 52–55)

elk 440mm (p. 56)

chipmunk
29-38mm
(p. 35–38)

8

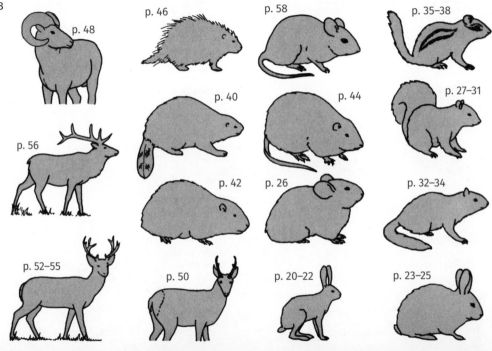

p. 19

p. 70

p. 39

p. 88

9

p. 18

p. 64–67

p. 74

p. 90

p. 76

p. 72

p. 68

p. 62

p. 80

p. 82–87

p. 78

skunk 30-44mm
(p. 64–67)

opossum 42mm (p. 62)

weasel 28mm (p. 72)

marten 70-95mm
(p. 70)

raccoon 30-50mm
(p. 76)

badger 34-49mm
(p. 74)

fox 31-69mm
(p. 82–87)

bobcat
50-127mm
(p. 88)

coyote 55-88mm
(p. 80)

cougar 76-228mm (p. 90)

bear 80–110mm (p. 78)

chipmunk 5–12mm
(p. 35–38)

pika 3–5mm (p. 26)

rabbits 5–10mm
(p. 23–25)

tree squirrel 9–14mm
(p. 27–31)

ground squirrel 10–14mm
(p. 32–34)

hares 10-13mm
(p. 20–22)

woodrat 10–14mm
(p. 58)

mt. beaver 15mm (p. 42)

marmot 28-40mm
(p. 39)

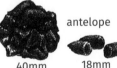
antelope

40mm   18mm
(p. 50)

12-28mm   48-67mm
deer (p. 52–55)

porcupine 35-47mm
(p. 46)

bighorn 80mm (p. 48)

elk (p. 56)

18-35mm

110mm

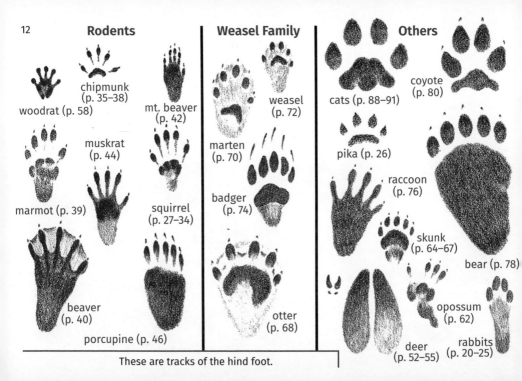

12

Rodents

woodrat (p. 58)

chipmunk (p. 35–38)

mt. beaver (p. 42)

muskrat (p. 44)

marmot (p. 39)

squirrel (p. 27–34)

beaver (p. 40)

porcupine (p. 46)

Weasel Family

weasel (p. 72)

marten (p. 70)

badger (p. 74)

otter (p. 68)

Others

cats (p. 88–91)

coyote (p. 80)

pika (p. 26)

raccoon (p. 76)

skunk (p. 64–67)

bear (p. 78)

opossum (p. 62)

deer (p. 52–55)

rabbits (p. 20–25)

These are tracks of the hind foot.

If you've found:

- a hole leading into a tunnel with an opening that is:
  - flat across the bottom, solitary, wider than 20 cm, often with smaller round holes nearby, see badger, p. 74.
  - round, wider than 20 cm, with similar ones nearby, in sandy soil of deserts and San Joaquin Valley, see kit fox, p. 82.
  - round, 10 cm or so across, in groups of several, on hillside or flat with little or no grass nearby, see ground squirrels, p. 32.
  - less than 6 cm in diameter, usually at base of shrub or tree, in mountainous area, with others nearby, see chipmunks p. 35.

- a linear ridge of soil, go to this symbol  below.
- a round mound of pushed-up soil, go to —————————————— next page.
- a nest or house of twigs, go to ※ next page.
- a depressed or matted-down area, go to —————————————— next page.

If the ridge is smooth, branched, on top of ground in snow country, spring/summer, see gopher, p. 18.

If the ridge appears pushed up or caved in, in lawn or soil, see mole, p. 19.

If a plugged tunnel is found under an edge of the mound, see gopher, p. 18.
If the mound has no obvious plugged tunnel entrance, see mole, p. 19.

If the nest is:

- among high or outer branches of tree, see tree squirrels, p. 27.
- a cone-shaped pile of twigs, 1–2 m high, at the base of trees, shrubs, in crevices, or back of caves, see woodrats, p. 58.
- a stack of cut grass piled under a rock ledge or among rock piles of high mountain areas, see pika, p. 26.
- made of matted cattails or other marsh plants, 1 m high, along stream or marsh edge, see muskrat, p. 44.
- made of stacked twigs in mounded piles 2–3 m high/wide, with mud packed on top, near twig dam, near or in water, see beaver, p. 40.

If the depression or matted area is:

- composed of tules, bulrushes, or streamside grasses, matted down, with tufts of twisted grass, droppings, musky odor, see river otter, p. 68.
- in grassland, chaparral, or next to rocks, brush, or bunchgrass, less than 0.5 m long, see rabbits/hares, p. 20–25.
- in meadow, forest, chaparral area, with or without strong urine scent and droppings, over 1 m long, see deer/elk, p 52–57.

If you've found:

- tree trunks/limbs with chew marks, gouges, or missing bark, go to this symbol below.

- tree trunks with vertical scratch or claw marks, go to next page.

- tips of tree/shrub branches nipped, pruned, or stripped of leaves, go to next page.

- chewed cones, nuts, or eucalyptus cones, go to next page.

- signs that don't fit into above categories, go to ———————— page 17.

If the chew marks or gouges are:

- Many, on one side or all around lower part of tree trunk, deep into wood, often felling tree, near pond, stream, see beaver, p. 40.

- large patches of bark removed, but not cut deeply into wood, often at several places on same tree, see porcupine, p. 46.

- linear gouges that break through the bark, but not deep into wood, extending several feet above the ground, see elk, p. 56.

- sharp, with shredded bark, 1 m or so aboveground, common on saplings, low branches, see deer/elk, p. 52–57.

- vertical, sharp, on underlying wood with bark torn away, 2 m or more aboveground, see bear, p. 78.

If you've found:

- chewed pine or spruce cones occurring in piles in mountainous area, see chickaree, p. 29.
- chewed eucalyptus fruit scattered under tree, see fox squirrel, p. 28.
- other cones or nuts in foothills or valleys, see fox or gray squirrel, p. 28, 30.

If the bark has claw-puncture marks that are:

- obvious, long, usually associated with extensive damage to tree, see bear, p. 78.
- in sets, under 6 cm wide, hard to find, see bobcat, p. 88.
- in sets, over 6 cm wide, hard to find, see mountain lion, p. 90.

If you've found:

- tips of shrub branches stripped of all leaves, see deer, p. 52–55.
- all of the lower branches of a tree pruned evenly and horizontally, 2–3 m aboveground, see deer/elk, p. 52–57.
- tips of small shrub branches under 1 m high nipped off at an angle, see rabbits/hares, p. 20–25.

If you've found:

- a dam of sticks across a stream forming a pond, see beaver, p. 40.
- piles of small pine or spruce cones next to logs or rocks, see chickaree, p. 29.
- a round, bowl-shaped hole in ground with wasp and paper nest parts scattered, see skunks, p. 64–67.
- long, muddy slides on riverbanks, see river otter, p. 68.
- partially buried droppings with scratches nearby, see bobcat, mountain lion, p. 88–91.
- tightly bound, twisted, cigar-shaped masses of foil, cellophane, or grass, see coyote, p. 80.
- any other signs, try a larger book. See p. 92.

Droppings
8mm, rarely found

$$\frac{1\ 0\ 1\ 3}{1\ 0\ 1\ 3}$$ 35–36mm

talpoides

bottae

mazama

Gopher esker: solid ridge on top of soil in snow country; no tunnel beneath

Pocket Gopher

Thomomys bottae, T. talpoides, T. mazama

Has large, external, fur-lined cheek pouches for carrying food. Squeezes contents out with forepaws; turns pouches inside out for cleaning. Burrowing area may cover 2,000 square feet. Gophers' lips close behind upper incisors to keep dirt out of their mouth while they dig. Enamel covers fronts of incisors, creating sharp, beveled edges as backs of teeth wear faster. Gophers are active day and night, year-round. Eats roots, tubers, greens. Solitary. Males fight other gophers on contact, except females in breeding season. Two species rarely live in same field. Sexually mature at 3 months. Young born mainly in spring, one or two litters per year, 2–11 per litter. Predation low. Enemies: badgers, weasels, snakes, owls, hawks, coyotes, foxes. Unlike other gophers, *T. mazama* spends time aboveground at night and on dark days, resulting in a higher predation rate.

Mole

Scapanus townsendii, S. latimanus, S. orarius

Fur blackish-brown or gray-brown, velvety, flexible; allows forward or backward movement in tunnels with equal ease. Eyes pinhead size. Earholes concealed. Naked nose is most vital sense organ. Mole digs with broad front feet in breaststroke motion. Can tunnel 30 cm per minute. Mounds appear to erupt from earth. Tunnel ridges collapse in time; improve soil aeration, rain penetration, reduce erosion. Feeds on worms, insects, centipedes, snails, slugs, some root crops. Young born March–April, two to six per litter. Active day and night. Rarely aboveground, thus low predation rate.

Mole tunnel: ridge of pushed-up soil or grass; may collapse

townsendii

orarius

latimanus

$$\frac{3\ 1\ 4\ 3}{3\ 1\ 4\ 3}$$

Skull lengths:
S. orarius 33–39mm (illus.)
S. townsendii 41–44mm
S. latimanus 29–37mm

Droppings are rarely found.

Black-tailed Jackrabbit
Black-tailed Hare
Lepus californicus

Gray-brown, tawny; common in sage, cactus, meadow, and open grassland country. Recognized by large black-tipped ears and habit of placing hind feet ahead of front feet in normal gait. Eyeshine is red. Feeds on green vegetation, shrubs, and cacti. Most active early evening and morning. Can run 30–35 mph. Uses a zigzag running escape pattern. Young are born year-round, furry, with eyes open. Enemies: coyotes, eagles, hawks, barn owls, large snakes.

All rabbits and hares form two kinds of droppings: soft, which are later ingested for vitamin and protein nutrition, and hard, which are not.

(skull illus. on p. 21)

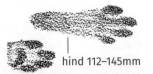

hind 112–145mm

10–12mm

White-tailed Jackrabbit, White-tailed Hare

Lepus townsendii

Gray-brown, often turns white in winter, but always has white tail with slight dorsal stripe. Ears narrower than those of black-tailed. Common in sagebrush and open areas; does not burrow. Can jump 5 m on a bound with speeds up to 40 mph. Feeds at night on sage, grass, and bark of young trees. Young born furry, with eyes open, three to six per annual litter. Enemies: foxes, coyotes, bobcats, lions, owls, hawks, eagles. Ears of all "Jacks" are long and well supplied with blood vessels to disperse body heat in hot weather.

Skull lengths:
Black-tailed 66–77mm
White-tailed 67–75mm
Snowshoe 53–56mm

$$\frac{2\ 0\ 3\ 3}{1\ 0\ 2\ 3}$$

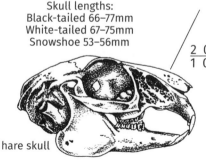

hare skull

18mm

Snowshoe Hare
Lepus americanus

Changes from dark brown in summer to white in winter. Only tips of hairs turn white. Eyeshine is orange. Found in swamps, forests, mountain thickets. Home range: 10 acres or more. Nocturnal. Feeds on succulent vegetation in summer; twigs, bark, buds, and sometimes frozen carcasses in winter. Does not build nest. Young born April–August, two to three litters per year, two to four per litter. Populations fluctuate dramatically, with peaks every 11 years or so. Life span: about 3 years in wild.

> **CAUTION:** All hares and rabbits may carry tularemia or "rabbit disease," which can be transmitted to people. Avoid handling dead rabbits, but, if necessary, use rubber gloves.

(skull illus. on p. 21)

hind 112–150mm

10–13mm

Brush Rabbit

Sylvilagus bachmani

Occupies chaparral and thick brush of coastal and foothill areas. Stays close to thickets, often clearing vegetation to bare ground along edges between brush and grass areas. Home range ¼–1 acre, with one to three rabbits per acre. Least active in middle of day, but feeds on vegetation anytime. Basks in morning sun. Young born with short, fine hair, but blind; two to six per litter, sometimes three to four litters per year, January–June. Same enemies as other rabbits; also vulnerable to dogs. Some tick species are specifically attracted to the ears of pregnant females for their blood meal, which provides the hormones the ticks need for reproduction.

(skull illus. on p. 24)

5–10mm

65–80mm

Mountain Cottontail
Sylvilagus nuttallii

Small, white-tailed, lives in brushy-rocky areas of juniper woodland, pinyon-juniper, and sagebrush desert areas. Long hairs in uniform-colored ears distinguish it from Audubon cottontail. Nocturnal, but also active in morning. Feeds on sagebrush, grass, and tree shoots. Young born naked, blind, in fur-lined nest in early summer, one to eight per litter. Rabbits in some areas produce several litters per year. Enemies same as other rabbits.

Skull lengths:
Brush 66–77mm
Mountain 67–75mm
Audubon 53–56mm

Skull illustrated is *S. auduboni*. Skulls of *S. bachmani* and *S. nuttallii* have different lattice work here.

7–9mm

(hind foot: 88–100mm, illus. on p. 23)

$$\frac{2\ 0\ 2\ 3}{1\ 0\ 2\ 3}$$

Audubon Cottontail
Desert Cottontail
Sylvilagus audubonii

Dark ear tips, larger size, and white-tipped hairs on underside distinguish it from brush rabbits. In open plains, foothills, low valleys, coastal areas; in grass, sage, pinyon-juniper, moist chaparral. Home range: 1 acre for females, up to 15 acres for males. Active in late afternoon, night, and early morning. Stays close to thickets. Eats green vegetation and a variety of fruit, but rarely tree bark. Young born naked and blind, in fur nests, throughout the year. May live 2 years in wild. Vulnerable to marauding domestic dogs.

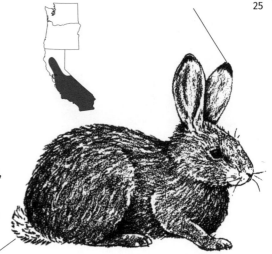

8mm

(skull illus. on p. 24)

hind 75–100mm

Pika, Cony, Rock Rabbit, Piping Hare
Ochotona princeps

Round body, short legs and ears, and dense fur conserve body heat. No visible tail. Common on alpine and fir forest talus slides. Variable color blends with rocks. Territorial. Presence indicated by its sharp, nasally chirps, and by hay piles of drying vegetation (each one may be a bushel or more). Diurnal. Does not hibernate. Active under snow, using stored hay for food. Ingests soft droppings for protein, energy, and vitamins. Stores dried marmot droppings for same use. Concentrates urine to conserve water; leaves distinctive white marks on rocks. Young born May–August, naked, blind, three to four per annual litter. Enemies: weasels, martens, coyotes, hawks. Currently threatened by climate change.

hind 25–35mm

25mm

3–5mm

40–45 mm

$$\frac{2 \quad 0 \quad 2 \quad 3}{1 \quad 0 \quad 2 \quad 3} \quad \text{or} \quad \frac{1 \quad 0 \quad 3 \quad 2}{1 \quad 0 \quad 2 \quad 3}$$

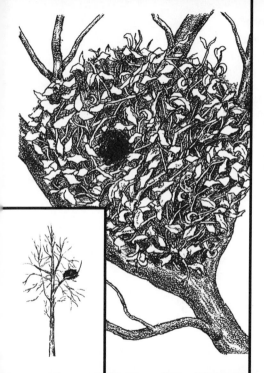

SQUIRRELS

There are about 11 species of ground and tree squirrels. Most do not hibernate but sleep for short periods. Eat variety of green vegetation, seeds, nuts, fruit, flowers, bulbs, roots, fungi, birds' eggs, insects, baby birds, and occasionally fresh roadkill. Most store food for use after awakening from sleep periods and in spring. Enemies include coyotes, foxes, bobcats, martens, fishers, weasels, hawks, owls, and large snakes.

Several species gnaw cones for nuts and sweet sap.

Fox Squirrel
Sciurus niger

Rusty, reddish-gray, lower parts rusty-yellow or orange; some pure gray, no rust. Melanistic forms occur. Introduced from east to city parks and campuses, now widespread in urban areas. Replaces native western gray squirrel as range extends. Like western gray squirrel, buries acorns and pine nuts, some of which are not retrieved and grow into trees. Young born February–July, two to four per litter, with two litters per year. Life span: about 7 years.

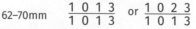

10–12mm

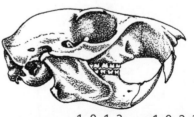

62–70mm $\frac{1\ 0\ 1\ 3}{1\ 0\ 1\ 3}$ or $\frac{1\ 0\ 2\ 3}{1\ 0\ 1\ 3}$

hind 50mm

Chickaree
Douglas Squirrel
Tamiasciurus douglasi

Dark olive-gray, grayer in winter, hairs sometimes red-tipped. Light yellowish or rusty belly. Black line along side is distinct in summer, less so in winter. Found in conifer forests in pine, spruce, fir, hemlock zones. Active all day. Very noisy. Feeds heavily on truffles and turpentine-flavored nuts of conifer cones. Stockpiles large numbers of pine cones near rocks and logs in fall for winter and spring use. One cache of 1,242 sequoia cones has been found. Young are born June–October, four to eight per litter, with one or two litters per year.

hind 5–55mm

6–10mm

47–50mm

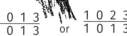

$\frac{1\ 0\ 1\ 3}{1\ 0\ 1\ 3}$ or $\frac{1\ 0\ 2\ 3}{1\ 0\ 1\ 3}$

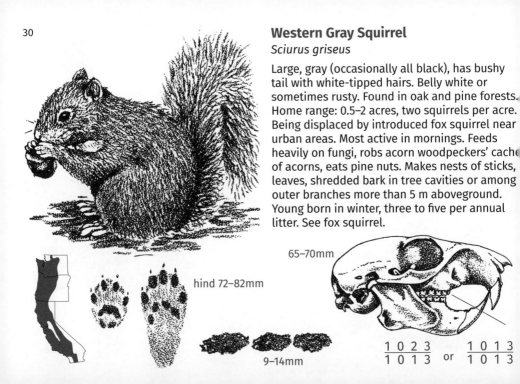

Western Gray Squirrel
Sciurus griseus

Large, gray (occasionally all black), has bushy tail with white-tipped hairs. Belly white or sometimes rusty. Found in oak and pine forests. Home range: 0.5–2 acres, two squirrels per acre. Being displaced by introduced fox squirrel near urban areas. Most active in mornings. Feeds heavily on fungi, robs acorn woodpeckers' cache of acorns, eats pine nuts. Makes nests of sticks, leaves, shredded bark in tree cavities or among outer branches more than 5 m aboveground. Young born in winter, three to five per annual litter. See fox squirrel.

hind 72–82mm

65–70mm

9–14mm

$$\frac{1\ 0\ 2\ 3}{1\ 0\ 1\ 3} \quad \text{or} \quad \frac{1\ 0\ 1\ 3}{1\ 0\ 1\ 3}$$

Northern Flying Squirrel
Glaucomys sabrinus

Body gray-brown, belly hairs white-tipped, with fur-covered skin membrane between fore and hind limbs used for gliding. Found in coniferous and mixed forests. Home range: about 4 acres. The only nocturnal squirrel. Eats lots of fungi in summer, lichens in winter. Gregarious in winter, may den in groups. Nests in old woodpecker holes or other tree cavities. Young born May–June, two to six per annual litter. Worst enemies: logging, owls.

hind 36–39mm

4–12mm

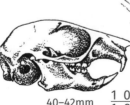

40–42mm $\frac{1\ 0\ 2\ 3}{1\ 0\ 1\ 3}$

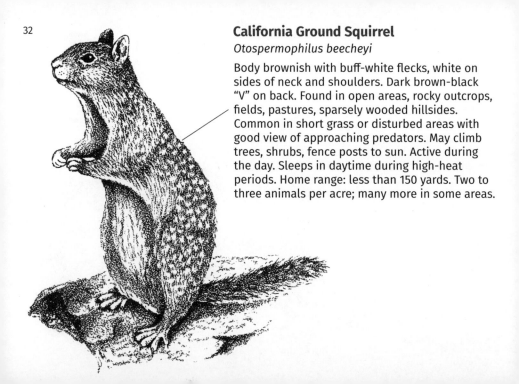

California Ground Squirrel
Otospermophilus beecheyi

Body brownish with buff-white flecks, white on sides of neck and shoulders. Dark brown-black "V" on back. Found in open areas, rocky outcrops, fields, pastures, sparsely wooded hillsides. Common in short grass or disturbed areas with good view of approaching predators. May climb trees, shrubs, fence posts to sun. Active during the day. Sleeps in daytime during high-heat periods. Home range: less than 150 yards. Two to three animals per acre; many more in some areas.

51–62mm

Hibernates November–February in snow country. Eats variety of vegetable matter, occasionally quail eggs, chicks, and fresh roadkill. Young born 4–15 per litter, spring–fall. Badgers and rattlesnakes are major enemies. In some parts of California, half of all young produced in a season are eaten by rattlesnakes. Ground squirrel fleas can carry bubonic plague.

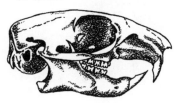

$$\frac{1 \quad 0 \quad 2 \quad 3}{1 \quad 0 \quad 1 \quad 3}$$

10–14mm

hind 50–64mm

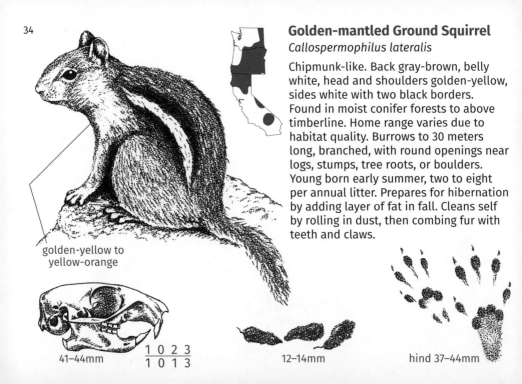

34

Golden-mantled Ground Squirrel
Callospermophilus lateralis

Chipmunk-like. Back gray-brown, belly white, head and shoulders golden-yellow, sides white with two black borders. Found in moist conifer forests to above timberline. Home range varies due to habitat quality. Burrows to 30 meters long, branched, with round openings near logs, stumps, tree roots, or boulders. Young born early summer, two to eight per annual litter. Prepares for hibernation by adding layer of fat in fall. Cleans self by rolling in dust, then combing fur with teeth and claws.

golden-yellow to
yellow-orange

41–44mm

$\dfrac{1\ 0\ 2\ 3}{1\ 0\ 1\ 3}$

12–14mm

hind 37–44mm

CHIPMUNKS

About 11 species in the Pacific states. Some are distinguishable only by bone characteristics, geography, habitat. All have internal cheek pouches for food gathering. All are diurnal. Instead of storing body fat like true hibernators, chipmunks store large quantities of food in burrows for use during waking periods and in early spring. Inactive for short periods. Gestation takes about one month. Young born in spring, two to seven per litter, usually one litter per year. Life span: about 5 years. Enemies: hawks, weasels, bobcats, coyotes, and snakes.

$$\frac{1\ 0\ 2\ 3}{1\ 0\ 1\ 3}$$

front

hind

Lengths of	skull	hind foot	dropping	
Least chipmunk	29–30mm	26–31mm	5–7mm	⎤ p. 36
Lodgepole	34–36mm	32–36mm	7mm	⎦
Merriam's	36–40mm	32–39mm	5–12mm	⎤ p. 37
Yellow pine	31–35mm	29–35mm	5–12mm	⎦
Townsend's	39mm	34–38mm	5–12mm	⎤ p. 38
Sonoma	36–39mm	33–37mm	5–12mm	⎦

Least Chipmunk
Tamias minimus

Color varies from yellowish-gray with tawny dark stripes to rich gray-tawny with black stripes. Sides often orange-brown. Lightest colored of all chipmunks. Found in low sagebrush deserts to high mountain conifer forests. Nests beneath stumps, logs, rocks, in ground. Lines burrow and nest with moss, lichens, grass, and feathers. Runs with tail up.

Lodgepole Chipmunk
Tamias speciosus

Brightly colored with light–dark contrasting colors, side stripes white and dark brown. Found in lodgepole pine forests, adjacent chaparral, red fir forests. Eats manzanita flowers, berries, nuts, fungi, and caterpillars.

Merriam's Chipmunk
Tamias merriami

Large, grayish-brown, with indistinct stripes. Found on chaparral slopes, in mixed-oak woodlands, bull pines, stream thickets, outcrops in foothills. Food similar to that of other chipmunks. Two color forms exist in range: those in humid areas tend to be darker than those in arid areas.

Yellow Pine Chipmunk
Tamias amoenus

Colors bright tawny to pink-cinnamon, black-and-white back and side stripes; ears black in front, white in back. Found in open conifer forests, chaparral, rocky areas with brush or pines. One cache of food contained 67,970 items with 15 different kinds of seeds, corn, and a piece of a bumblebee.

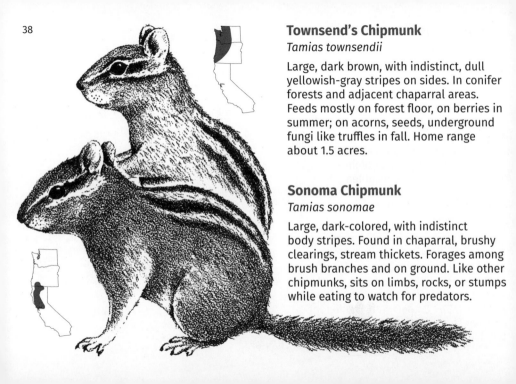

Townsend's Chipmunk
Tamias townsendii

Large, dark brown, with indistinct, dull yellowish-gray stripes on sides. In conifer forests and adjacent chaparral areas. Feeds mostly on forest floor, on berries in summer; on acorns, seeds, underground fungi like truffles in fall. Home range about 1.5 acres.

Sonoma Chipmunk
Tamias sonomae

Large, dark-colored, with indistinct body stripes. Found in chaparral, brushy clearings, stream thickets. Forages among brush branches and on ground. Like other chipmunks, sits on limbs, rocks, or stumps while eating to watch for predators.

Yellow-bellied Marmot
Marmota flaviventris

Heavy-bodied rodent common on talus slopes and roadside rock piles in high mountains. Shares habitat with pikas. Body yellow-brown. All-black individuals occur. Burrow entrance to 23 cm wide, with fan of packed dirt. Marmot dens in talus pile. Nearby large boulder is used as lookout. Chirps or whistles when alarmed. Often in colonies with a dominant male who may have harem of several females. Eats green vegetation. Diurnal. Develops layer of fat for hibernation October–March. One litter of three to six blind, naked young born late spring. Life span: about 15 years. Enemies: eagles, coyotes, bobcats, lions.

$$\frac{1\ 0\ 2\ 3}{1\ 0\ 1\ 3}$$

80–91mm

28–40mm

hind 70–90mm

Beaver
Castor canadensis

Large, dark-brown rodent with scaly tail. Skull has chestnut-brown incisors. Lives in mountain streams, ponds, lakes. Its transparent eyelids cover eyes during dives to allow continuous vision while underwater. When alarmed, it slaps water with its tail as a warning to other beavers. Gnaws trees until they fall: for food; for building materials for bow-shaped dams and domelike lodges; and for scent mounds, which mark territory and attract mates. Burrows up through snow to gnaw trees at surface; as snow level changes, several gnawed bands may be left, creating a totem pole effect. Active throughout year. Feeds mostly on aspen, cottonwood, willow, and birch. Will also eat cattails, tules, willow roots, pond lilies. Its droppings of coarse, sawdust-like material are rarely found because they decompose rapidly. Probably mates for life. Kits born furry, eyes open, four per litter. Stay with parents for two years. Life span: 10–12 years. Young killed by otters. Adults occasionally killed by coyotes, foxes, bobcats, and lions. Almost trapped to extinction in 19th century to supply soft, fine fur for hats, robes, and coats; now reestablished over most of its former range.

113–130mm

$$\frac{1\ 0\ 1\ 3}{1\ 0\ 1\ 3}$$

hind 165mm   top view of molar

Droppings: 35–40mm, rarely found

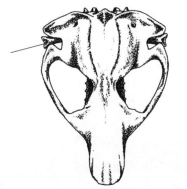

56–62mm

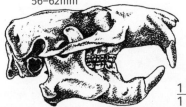

$$\frac{1\ 0\ 2\ 3}{1\ 0\ 1\ 3}$$

Mountain Beaver
Aplodontia rufa

Dark brown above, lighter below, nearly tailless. Not really a beaver. Its burrow entrances, to 20 cm across, sometimes have a tent of twigs covered with leaves and fern fronds erected over them. Nips branches near burrow entrances. Its tunnels are shallow, prone to collapsing, often leading to food and water. Eats mostly bark and ferns (especially bracken and swordfern); creates hay piles to dry plants for nests and food. Ingests own droppings. Active at night, autumn days. Climbs trees. Voice a shrill whistle, rarely heard. Females breed at 2 years; one litter of three to five is born in spring. Enemies: bobcats, long-tailed weasels, mink.

15mm

hind 55–63

no visible tail

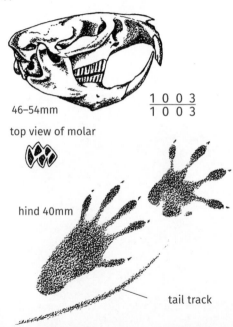

46–54mm

$$\frac{1\ 0\ 0\ 3}{1\ 0\ 0\ 3}$$

top view of molar

hind 40mm

tail track

Muskrat

Ondatra zibethicus

Aquatic rodent with dark-brown, glossy fur. Naked tail is flattened vertically for swimming. Excellent swimmer; can stay submerged for 15 minutes. Mouth closes behind protruding incisors, making underwater chewing possible. Builds house of matted vegetation to 1.2 m high; burrows in banks; makes feeding platforms. Marks territory with mats of cut plants where scent is spread. Active day and night. Eats aquatic plants, clams, crayfish, frogs, fish. Breeds April–August, has up to five litters per year of four to seven naked, blind young. Babies swim at 1 week. Life span: 5–6 years. Raccoons, otters, mink, and people are major enemies.

Droppings: 10–13mm, rarely found

46

Porcupine
Erethizon dorsatus

Gray-brown, chunky body, high-arching back, short legs. Has about 30,000 hair quills on back, rump, and tail. When alarmed, flips tail, releasing quills from skin. Quills are not thrown. Once in an enemy's flesh, the quills work deeper and can be fatal. Porcupine has no other defense. Found in forests and some open areas. Active year-round. Mostly nocturnal, but suns in trees. Solitary in summer, lives colonially in winter. Eats green plants and inside layer of tree bark. Fond of salt. Mates in fall. One baby born May or June, headfirst, with soft quills aimed backward. Fishers circle porcupines, biting at face until able to inflict mortal wound. Mountain lions, coyotes, bobcats also attack them.

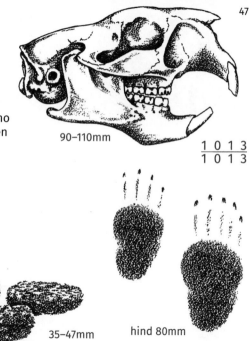

90–110mm

$$\frac{1 \quad 0 \quad 1 \quad 3}{1 \quad 0 \quad 1 \quad 3}$$

hind 80mm

35–47mm

quill magnified

48

Bighorn Sheep
Ovis canadensis

Gray-brown to ash-gray; belly, rump white. Horns on rams thick, coiled; in ewes, not coiled, small. Sexes separate in summer, together in fall. Rams of equal size challenge each other for ewes; rear and charge at 20 mph to butt heads loudly. Skull is double thick with struts of bone to cushion impact. Eats sedge, grass, sagebrush, alpine plants. Bed is a depression smelling of urine with droppings along edges, used for years. Single lamb born May–June; stays with herd. Lives 14 years. Golden eagles take lambs. Threatened by weather, disease, loss of viable habitat, intrusion. Several isolated races or populations occur.

bone core without horn sheath

with horn sheath

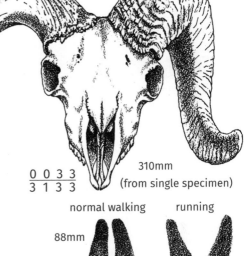

$$\frac{0\ \ 0\ \ 3\ \ 3}{3\ \ 1\ \ 3\ \ 3}$$

310mm
(from single specimen)

normal walking   running

88mm

13–16mm

cakes: 80mm

dew claws —

50

normal walking   running

70mm

cakes: 40mm

pellets: 18mm

Pronghorn Antelope

Antilocapra americana

Upper body tan; chest, belly, rump white. Short, erect mane. Antelope raises rump hairs to flash warning when alarmed. Sheds outer covering of horns after breeding season; permanent core remains. Can run at 44 mph, with short bursts to 70 mph—fastest animal in western hemisphere. Can leap horizontally 4–8 m, but can't jump fences. Found in open prairies and sagebrush plains. Forms summer bands up to 12 animals; winter bands up to 100. Eats grasses, cacti, sagebrush, rabbitbrush. Droppings are in segmented masses when antelope eats succulent grass, small pebble-like forms when it browses. Breeds in fall. Young born April–June, unspotted, odorless. Twins common. Life span: about 10 years. Chief enemy: coyotes.

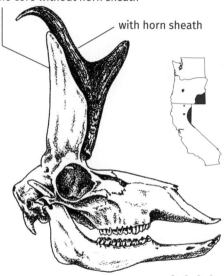

bone core without horn sheath

with horn sheath

290mm
(from single specimen)

$$\frac{0\ \ 0\ \ 3\ \ 3}{3\ \ 1\ \ 3\ \ 3}$$

Mule Deer

Odocoileus hemionus

Coat varies: yellow-brown, sooty-gray, blue-gray. Tail white with black tip to all black. Rump patch white. Weighs 100–300 pounds. Antlers: branched; number of branches and rack size increase with age, decline after peak; are shed in winter; grown again in early spring; are covered with velvet until late summer. Buck damages saplings and branches by rubbing off velvet. Mule deer are active most hours except midday. Chiefly a browser; fond of clover, alfalfa, acorns, many shrubs.

Coastal deer lose weight June–November, followed by natural die-off. Survivors gain weight after fall rains. Shrubs resprouting after fires in the fall, combined with available acorns, supply deer with essential food for recovery.

Bucks solitary; may form bands before and after mating season. Harems form in

pellets: 12–18mm

cakes: 67mm

October. Spotless, odorless fawns are born May–June, hidden for one month. Young does have singles, older does have twins. Fawns, yearlings travel in family groups with mothers. Bucks urinate in beds as they stand; does step to one side first. Chief enemies: mountain lions, bobcats, coyotes, domestic dogs, people, and cars.

winter

spring

summer
(in velvet)

Six subspecies recognized by tail differences:

California Southern Inyo Rocky Mt. Burro Columbian Black-tailed

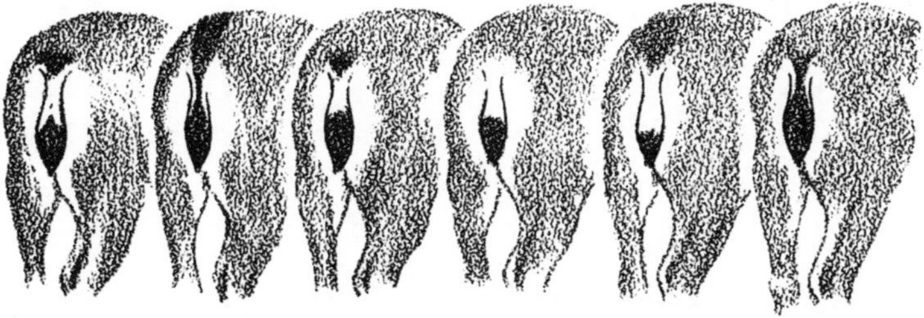

Illustration based on one in *Big Game of California*, see p. 92.

54

Mule Deer

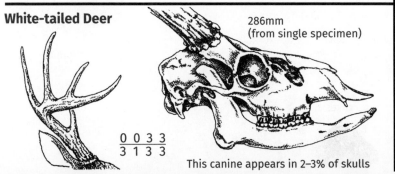

250mm
(from single specimen)

$$\frac{0\ 0\ 3\ 3}{3\ 1\ 3\ 3}$$

*Corner incisiform tooth in deer and elk is technically a canine.

White-tailed Deer

286mm
(from single specimen)

$$\frac{0\ 0\ 3\ 3}{3\ 1\ 3\ 3}$$

This canine appears in 2–3% of skulls

Mule and
White-tailed

running

dew claws

walking

63–82mm

White-tailed Deer
Odocoileus virginianus

Coat reddish in summer, blue-gray in winter. Raises all-white tail when running. Found in forests, brushlands, swampy meadowlands. Home range: about 1 mile. Runs to 40 mph. Jumps 9 m horizontally, 2.4 m high. Bucks rub antlers on tree trunks and saplings close to ground to mark territory, remove velvet, and to sharpen them. Breed November–February. Adult does often have twins. Stamps feet and snorts when nervous. Lives up to 16 years in wild. Rips vegetation away, rather than nipping as rabbits do. Same enemies as other deer. Two subspecies in the Pacific Coast area.

pellets: 12–28mm   cakes: 48mm

56

C. canadensis   C. nannodes

chew marks

Wapiti, Canadian Elk
Cervus elaphus canadensis

Tule Elk
C. elaphus nannodes

$$\frac{0\ \ 1\ \ 3\ \ 3}{3\ \ 1\ \ 3\ \ 3}$$

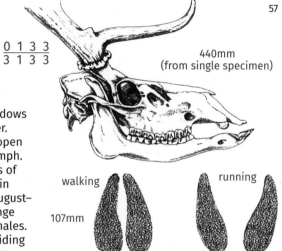

440mm
(from single specimen)

Tail and rump patch are tawny in wapiti; white in tule elk. Males to 1,000 pounds, females smaller. Habitat: mountain meadows in summer, lower wooded areas in winter. Tule elk prefer marshes, river bottoms, open plains. Active dusk to dawn. Can run 35 mph. Primarily grazers. Found in mixed groups of 25 or so in winter. Older bucks separate in summer. During breeding season (rut) August–November, bucks bugle loudly to challenge rivals and gather harems of up to 60 females. Bulls weakened after breeding go into hiding to avoid predators. Shed antlers February–March; new antlers start in April. Mountain lion is chief enemy. Bears and coyotes take calves. Wapiti were once slaughtered for their two upper canine "bugler" teeth, which were used for watch charms.

walking

running

107mm

dew claws

pellets: 18–35mm

cakes: 110mm

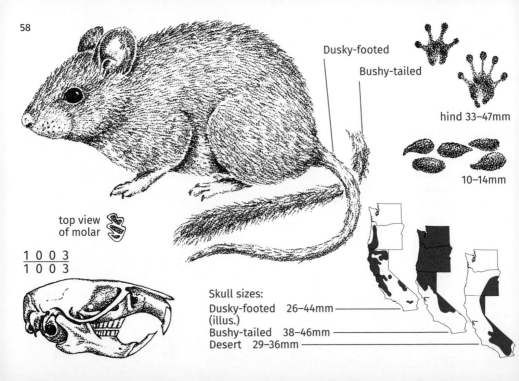

58

Dusky-footed

Bushy-tailed

hind 33–47mm

10–14mm

top view
of molar

$$\frac{1\ 0\ 0\ 3}{1\ 0\ 0\ 3}$$

Skull sizes:
Dusky-footed   26–44mm
(illus.)
Bushy-tailed   38–46mm
Desert   29–36mm

WOODRATS

Presence of gray-tawny woodrats is indicated by bulky nests of twigs at bases of trees, shrubs, in rock crevices, in cactus or tree branches. Earn name "packrat" by stashing anything they fancy in their nests. Nocturnal and territorial; they respond to disturbance by drumming or thumping with hind feet or tails. Woodrat tails have hairs, unlike old-world rats. Feed on green plants, nuts, seeds, fruit, fungi. Most species give birth to one to four young per annual litter. Enemies: owls, foxes, coyotes, bobcats, large snakes.

Desert woodrat (*Neotoma lepida*) may have four litters per year. It defends prickly pear patches for food and water during the dry season.

Dusky-footed woodrat (*N. fuscipes*) often builds a second escape nest in tree branches near ground nest.

Bushy-tailed woodrat (*N. cinerea*) accumulates various materials in rock crevices or under logs in high mountain areas.

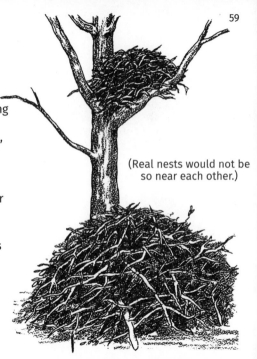

(Real nests would not be so near each other.)

Pallid Bat

$$\frac{1\ 1\ 1\ 3}{2\ 1\ 2\ 3}$$

Dental formulas vary
among bat species.

19–24mm

2–3mm

BATS

The Pacific Coast area has 25 species. Only true flying mammals. Furry bodies, naked wings. Hearing is acute. To avoid objects and locate food, bats depend on emission of sounds from nose or mouth, at rate of 30–60 squeaks per second, that echo back off objects. Muscles control ears so that bats hear only returning sound waves when flying. Bats capture insects in flight or on ground, consuming tons of destructive pests. Drink from streams, ponds, lakes in flight; often captured by large trout and bass. Feed around city streetlights; hang on porch walls and eat large insects, leaving droppings on walls. Hang head down. Metabolism lowered when asleep to conserve energy. Some bats are solitary, while others are colonial. Some migrate; others hibernate. One or two young born late spring.

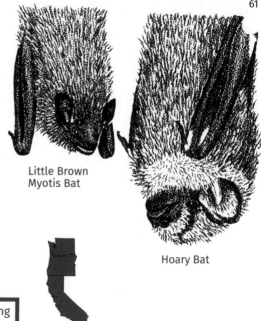

Little Brown Myotis Bat

Hoary Bat

CAUTION: Some bats carry rabies, so handling them is dangerous.

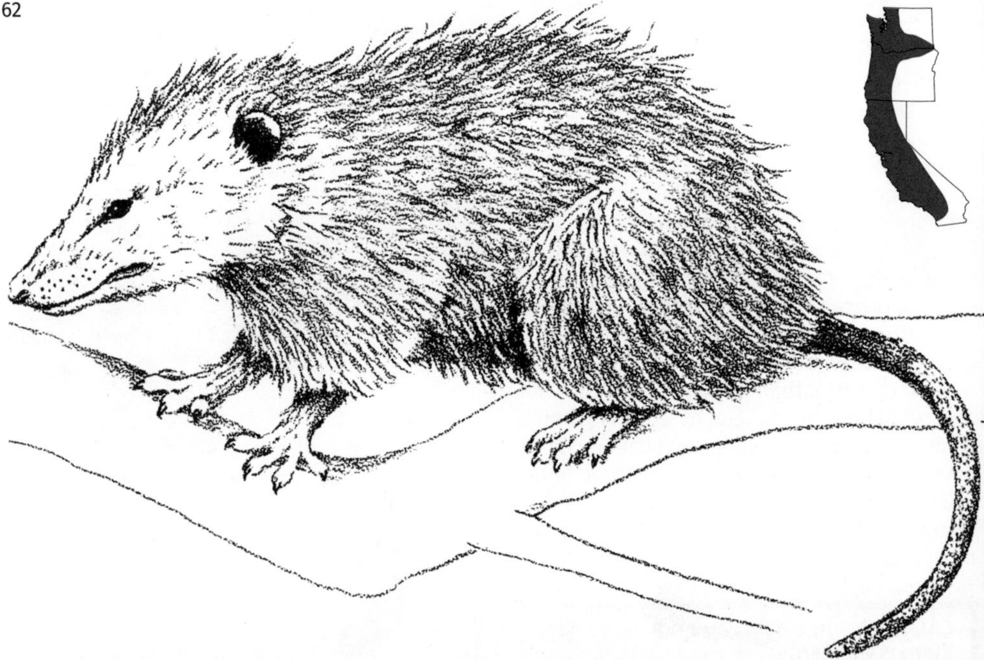

Opossum
Didelphis marsupialis

Only pouched mammal in US. Scruffy, gray body with prehensile tail. Thin, black, hairless ears and part of tail may be missing in north range, due to freezing. Opossum feigns death when threatened. Thrives in urban, rural, and woodland areas. Nests in hollow trees, logs, culverts, brush piles, under houses. Eats fruit, vegetables, nuts, insects, carrion, eggs. Nocturnal. Solitary. Does not hibernate; stays in den for several weeks in cold weather. Has one to two litters, January–October; 1–14 embryos crawl out of womb to pouch, covering 13 teats. All could fit in a teaspoon. Nurse for 2 months. Seven or fewer normally survive to juvenile stage. Life span: to 7 years.

hind 60–79mm

116–127mm

$$\frac{5}{4} \frac{1}{1} \frac{3}{3} \frac{4}{4}$$

small brain case

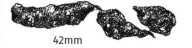

42mm

Spotted Skunk
Spilogale gracilis

Boldly marked, with pom-pom–like tail. More active than other skunks. Stands on front feet with back and tail arched over head as defense warning. Climbs trees to escape enemies. One spotted skunk may range over 160 acres. Less territorial than other skunks, more socially tolerant, thus 13 or more spotted skunks may be found in a square mile. Nests in burrows beneath buildings, rock piles. Several may den together in winter. Feeds on mice, birds, eggs, insects, carrion, and some vegetable matter. Mates in September. Two to seven young born May–June. Great horned owls, cars are worst enemies; foxes and bobcats harm a few.

hind 39–55mm

$$\frac{3\ 1\ 3\ 1}{3\ 1\ 3\ 2}$$

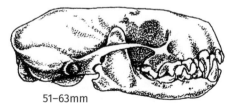

51–63mm

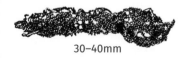

30–40mm

large space

hind 65–88m

69–87mm

$$\frac{3}{3} \frac{1}{1} \frac{3}{3} \frac{1}{2}$$

Striped Skunk
Mephitis mephitis

Bold coloring warns predators. When threatened, may snarl, stamp feet, raise hind legs, click teeth, arch tail, turn toward enemy. This failing, it shoots a jet spray of musk (to 4.5 m) as final defense. Adult skunk needs about 10 acres. Uses abandoned burrows of other animals, digs its own, or may use protected spaces under houses (unless repelled by mothballs). Nocturnal. Does not hibernate; may be inactive for weeks in winter. Males solitary; females may den together in winter. Eats variety of vegetable matter, insects, grubs, mice, eggs, frogs, and also yellowjackets and their nests, leaving large holes in ground. Four to seven young born in May, follow mother single file until June or July. Chief carrier of rabies. Predators: great horned owls, golden eagles.

30–44mm

River Otter

Lontra canadensis

Color rich brown above, silvery below. Can stay underwater 2–3 minutes because pulse slows and skin flaps close ears and nostrils. Lives in large rivers, streams, sloughs, or along seashore in northern areas. Home range: 15 miles. Travels at night. Enlarges and uses burrows of other animals, such as beavers and muskrats, for dens along water's edge. Makes riverbank slides 30 cm wide. Snow slides show track marks. When on land, spends most of its time frolicking, chasing tail, or playing tag. Rolls in tules or grass to dry off and to mark territory with musk, droppings. Females breed again just after giving birth, March–May, to one to four blind, helpless, furry pups that must be taught to swim. Eats fish.

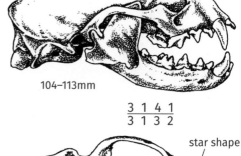

104–113mm

$$\frac{3}{3} \frac{1}{1} \frac{4}{3} \frac{1}{2}$$

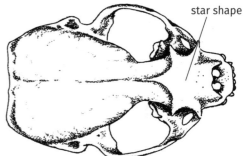

star shape

hind 100–146mm

Droppings: 60–65mm, rarely found

Pine Marten

Martes americana

Brown body with orange-yellow throat and chest. Lives in deep coniferous forests, large high-mountain rock piles. Dens in hollow trees. Active night, early morning, late afternoon, and cloudy days. Spends lots of time in trees. May range 15 miles in search of food. Eats tree squirrels, mice, voles, pikas, hares, some berries. Buries surplus meat. Breeds in midsummer; fertilization of eggs by sperm is delayed; embryos form in early winter. Young born in April, one to five in a litter. May breed after first year. Males use scent glands under belly skin to mark territory and attract mates. Martens are curious. One male was live-trapped 77 times in a row. Enemies: fishers, large owls.

72–83mm

$$\frac{3\ \ 1\ \ 4\ \ 1}{3\ \ 1\ \ 4\ \ 2}$$

Members of weasel family often show 1-3-1 placement of toes in track pattern.

55mm

hind 70–95mm

Long-tailed Weasel
Mustela frenata

Body brown, with black face and tail tip, underparts beige-yellow, except in snow country, northern areas, where shorter fall days stimulate color change to all white with black nose, eyes, and tail tip. Habitat varied: forest, brush, farmland, near water. Chiefly nocturnal, but active day and night, year-round. Eats mostly mice—often caches several dead mice under log. Also eats rabbits, squirrels, chipmunks, birds, etc. A ferocious and efficient mammal predator. Leaves droppings on logs, rocks, stumps. Lines nest, in abandoned den of other animal, with fur of mice and "trophies" (bones, feathers) of hunts. Three to nine nearly naked, blind young are normally born in May. Enemies: hawks, owls, cats, coyotes, foxes, mink, martens, fishers.

50mm (from one specimen)

$$\frac{3\ 1\ 3\ 1}{3\ 1\ 3\ 2}$$

hind 35–47mm

28mm

Badger

Taxidea taxus

Coat yellow–grizzled gray. Poor eyesight but strong senses of smell and hearing. Loose skin allows twisting, turning in tight spaces to catch food, defend self. Found in arid grassland in nearly all life zones. Digs to catch food, escape, rest, den, and bury droppings and extra food. Its burrow entrance is 20–30 cm wide, elliptical, with flat bottom. Eats rabbits, gophers, squirrels, mice, rattlesnakes, yellowjackets. Coyotes may follow badgers to steal the prey they flush from burrows. Badger is solitary, active day or night. May sleep for weeks during cold weather. Changes dens almost daily in summer. One to five cubs born blind, furry, February–May. Enemies are bears and lions, who do not find badgers easy prey. Their squat forms, sharp teeth, and strong neck muscles are major defensive tools.

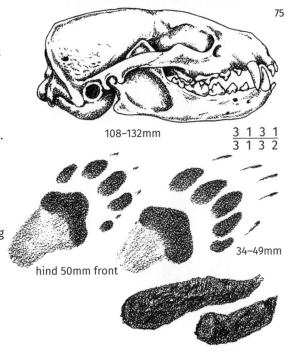

108–132mm

$$\frac{3\ 1\ 3\ 1}{3\ 1\ 3\ 2}$$

34–49mm

hind 50mm front

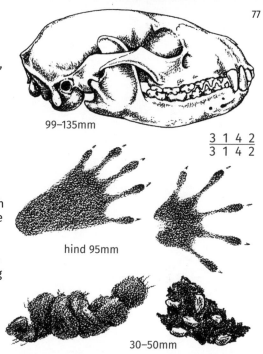

Raccoon
Procyon lotor

Salt-and-pepper color. Playful, curious, good swimmer. Feeds mostly along streams, lakes, ponds but will wander from water. Dens in hollow trees, logs, rock crevices, or ground burrows. In cold weather, may sleep for several days; does not hibernate. Chiefly nocturnal but occasionally about in the daytime. Especially active in autumn. Solitary, except when breeding, caring for young. Varied diet includes fruits, nuts, grains, insects, frogs, fish, crayfish, birds' eggs. Washing food enhances sense of touch in toes and helps raccoon discern nonedible matter. Leaves droppings at base of den tree, on large branches, rocks, logs across streams. Mates in February or March. Two to seven young born April or May. In fall, young raccoons may disperse up to 160 miles but mostly fewer than 30 miles. Chief enemies: dogs, hunters, cars. Can defend self well against a single dog.

99–135mm

$$\frac{3\ 1\ 4\ 2}{3\ 1\ 4\ 2}$$

hind 95mm

30–50mm

claw marks

78

Black Bear
Ursus americanus

Body black or cinnamon. Has keen sense of smell, climbs trees easily. Can run 30 mph in short bursts. Can range 15 miles. Dens under downed trees, hollow logs or trees, other shelter. Solitary, except when breeding and in garbage dumps. Mainly vegetarian but also eats fish, small mammals, eggs, carrion, honeycomb, bees, garbage. May sleep/den for periods, depending on stored fat and severity of winter. In fall, bears add thick layer of fat to sustain them during winter sleep; bears without enough fat are active during winter. Mates June–July, every other year. Two to three cubs born in winter den. Life span: 30 years. "Bear trees" have tooth marks as high as bear stands, claw marks above, to mark territory. Bears are dangerous when surprised, hungry, feeding, injured, or with cubs.

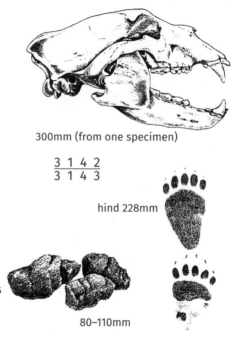

300mm (from one specimen)

$$\frac{3\ 1\ 4\ 2}{3\ 1\ 4\ 3}$$

hind 228mm

80–110mm

80

hind 57mm

Coyote

Canis latrans

Color and size variable. Mountain coyotes are larger, have longer fur than desert coyotes. Coyote is vocal at night—a series of yaps, a long howl, then short yaps. Holds tail between legs when running. Can reach 40 mph. Track like a dog's. Population, range increasing despite hunting, poisoning campaigns. Widespread. Dens along riverbanks, well-drained sides of canyons, gulches. May enlarge badger or squirrel burrows. Chiefly nocturnal but active anytime. Often hunts in pairs. Omnivorous but mostly eats small rodents, rabbits, squirrels. Droppings gray, with some seeds, but mostly fur, bones, insect parts, reptile skin, feathers; occasionally solid foil, plastic, or grass, which helps remove tapeworms. Mates January–March with six to seven pups born March–May; raised by both parents. Livestock losses blamed on coyotes are often the work of dogs. Coyotes kill many grass-eating rodents, earning protection from some ranchers.

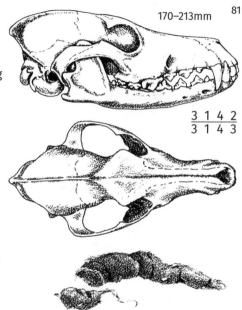

170–213mm

$$\frac{3\ 1\ 4\ 2}{3\ 1\ 4\ 3}$$

Droppings: gray-white with fur, bones, insect parts, 55–88mm long, 20mm diam.

82

hind 44mm

San Joaquin Kit Fox

Vulpes macrotis

Color sandy, tawny-gray. Mainly nocturnal but active during daytime in deserts. Hot weather forces it into burrow, 23 cm across, which it digs for itself in sandy soil, or it uses abandoned badger's den. Eats rodents, rabbits, insects, lizards, snakes. Uses stalk-and-pounce strategy. Very quick, running up to 25 mph. Four to five pups born February–March. Both parents raise young; while female cares for them, male hunts and returns with food. Family disperses in autumn. Eagles and coyotes are main enemies. In San Joaquin Valley, this fox is chief predator of rodents on agricultural land. Poison baits intended for coyotes kill many foxes, and their loss results in survival of high numbers of rodents that damage crops.

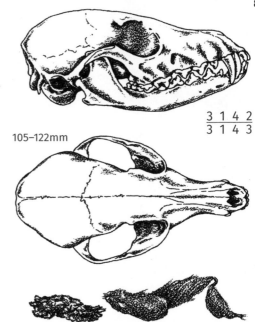

$\frac{3\ 1\ 4\ 2}{3\ 1\ 4\ 3}$

105–122mm

Droppings: 31–69mm, may resemble those of gray fox.

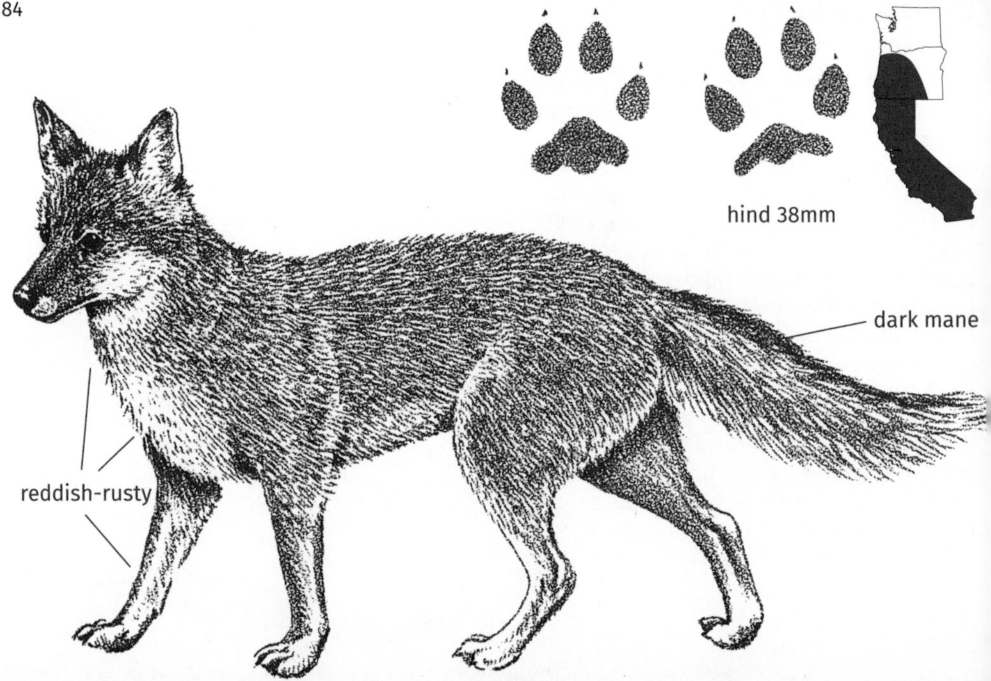

84

hind 38mm

dark mane

reddish-rusty

Gray Fox
Urocyon cinereoargenteus

Salt-and-pepper gray with rusty neck, legs, feet. Less vocal than other foxes. Can run, in short bursts, 28 mph. Only fox that climbs trees to escape or to hunt. Found mainly in woodland, chaparral. Dens in hollow trees, logs, under rock ledges, or in culverts; may have several escape dens nearby. Den area often marked by accumulation of droppings, bones. Nocturnal but often seen in daytime. Eats small rodents, insects, birds, eggs, fruit, acorns; in some areas, diet is largely cottontail rabbits, ground squirrels, berries. Two to seven pups are born March–April, dark brown, eyes closed. Hunt on their own at 4 months. Afflicted with many diseases, parasitic worms. Enemies: domestic dogs, bobcats, mountain lions, people. Poison bait intended for coyotes kills many gray foxes.

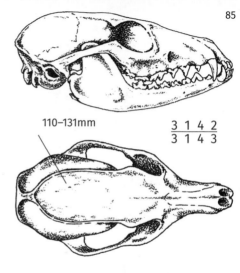

110–131mm

$$\frac{3 \quad 1 \quad 4 \quad 2}{3 \quad 1 \quad 4 \quad 3}$$

Droppings: 50mm, 10mm diam., smaller than coyote's, almost always black with stringy ends, berry seeds, fur, etc.

hind 50mm

white

nearly black legs/feet

Red Fox

Vulpes vulpes

Rusty-red, but several color phases exist. White-tipped tail a key feature. Found in cultivated land, wooded areas, brushland, high mountains. Range is expanding. Mostly nocturnal but also active early morning and evening. Eats fruit, insects, crayfish in summer; birds, mice, rabbits, squirrels in winter. Adults remain solitary until breeding time. Den usually in open area or along stream, in rock pile. May use enlarged den of badger or marmot. Entrance is 1 foot wide, with fan of packed dirt, bones, droppings; one to three smaller, less-conspicuous escape holes nearby. Establishes den after mating January–February; abandons it by late August when family disperses. Four to eight pups born March–May. After several weeks, parents deliver live prey so pups can practice killing. Young males disperse up to 150 miles from birthplace. Enemies: bobcats, coyotes, golden eagles, people.

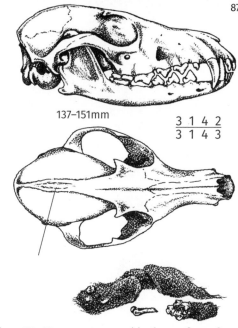

137–151mm

$$\frac{3\ 1\ 4\ 2}{3\ 1\ 4\ 3}$$

Droppings: 50–63mm, may resemble those of gray fox.

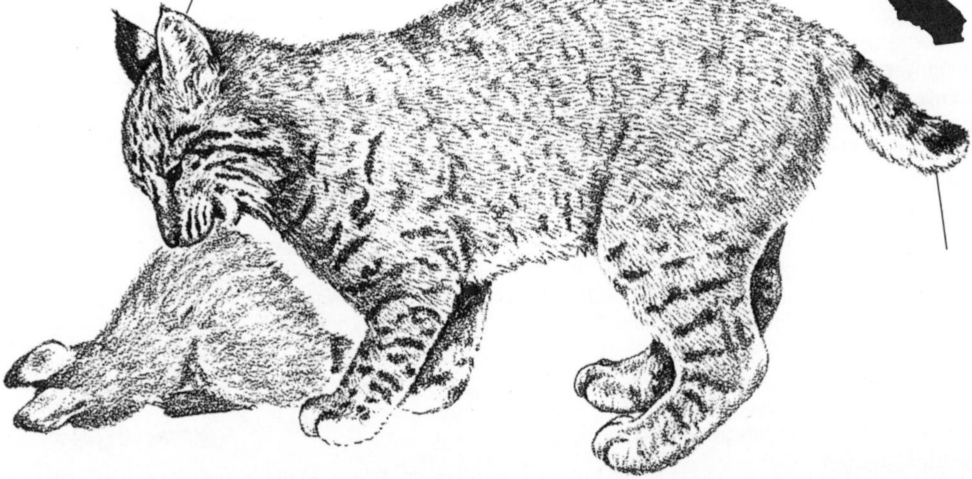

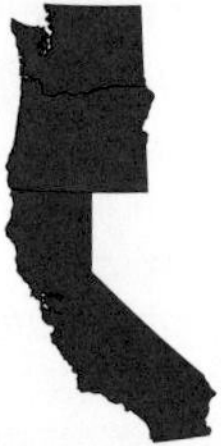

Bobcat
Lynx rufus

Gray-brown to reddish. Ear tufts used like antennae to aid hearing. Good climber. Gets name from bobbed tail. In almost every habitat, life zone. Range is usually within 2 miles but may be up to 50 miles. Mostly nocturnal but also seen in daytime. Solitary. Often rests on branches, atop large rocks to watch for passing prey. Eats rabbits, mice, squirrels, porcupines, woodrats, cave bats, small/weak deer. Caches large kills. Droppings are like dog's or coyote's but often partially buried, with scratch marks on ground. One to seven (average two to three) kittens born April–May in den of dry leaves in hollow log or under rock ledge or fallen tree. Southern animals may have two litters per year. Life span: to 25 years. Marks territory by urinating on rocks or tree trunks, making scent posts. Uses tree trunk as scratching post. Often killed by poison bait intended for coyotes.

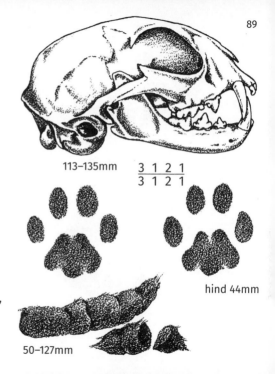

113–135mm

$$\frac{3\ 1\ 2\ 1}{3\ 1\ 2\ 1}$$

hind 44mm

50–127mm

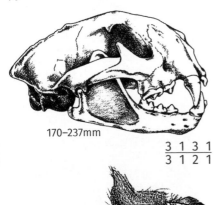

170–237mm

$$\frac{3\ 1\ 3\ 1}{3\ 1\ 2\ 1}$$

Droppings: 76–228mm. Form pellet droppings in desert. All cat droppings are partially buried.

Mountain Lion, Cougar, Puma
Puma concolor

Yellowish, grayish, reddish-tawny. Habitat generally wilderness but may hunt in rural hills. Male may travel 25 miles in one night. Strongly territorial. Mostly nocturnal. Rarely seen. Voice like tomcat's, greatly magnified. Uses tree trunks as scratching posts. Solitary, except for short breeding period. Eats large mammals; one deer per week forms half of diet. Has more success catching old, weak, less-alert deer, thus keeps herd healthy. Also eats coyotes, porcupines, beavers, rabbits, marmots, raccoons, birds, sometimes livestock. Covers remains of large kill with branches, leaves. Droppings often left like bobcat's. Adults breed every two–three years. One to six furry, spotted kittens born midsummer, raised by female for one to two years. Only enemy is man. The California Department of Fish and Wildlife considers lions as a **"specially protected species."** The population appears to be stable, with a rough estimate of 4,000–6,000 animals in the state, which could be seriously impacted by recent wildfires.

hind 101mm

INDEX

Other books in the pocket-size *Finder* series:

FOR US AND CANADA EAST OF THE ROCKIES

Berry Finder native plants with fleshy fruits
Bird Finder frequently seen birds
Bird Nest Finder aboveground nests
Fern Finder native ferns of the Midwest and Northeast
Flower Finder spring wildflowers and flower families
Life on Intertidal Rocks organisms of the
North Atlantic Coast
Scat Finder mammal scat
Track Finder mammal tracks and footprints
Tree Finder native and common introduced trees
Winter Tree Finder leafless winter trees
Winter Weed Finder dry plants in winter

FOR THE PACIFIC COAST

Pacific Coast Bird Finder frequently seen birds
Pacific Coast Fish Finder marine fish of the Pacific Coast
Pacific Coast Tree Finder native trees, from Sitka to
San Diego

FOR THE PACIFIC COAST (continued)

Pacific Intertidal Life organisms of the
Pacific Coast
Redwood Region Flower Finder
wildflowers of the coastal fog belt of CA

FOR ROCKY MOUNTAIN AND DESERT STATES

Desert Tree Finder desert trees of CA, AZ, NM
Rocky Mountain Flower Finder wildflowers
below tree line
Rocky Mountain Mammal Finder mammals, their tracks,
skulls, and other signs
Rocky Mountain Tree Finder native Rocky
Mountain trees

FOR STARGAZERS

Constellation Finder patterns in the night sky
and star stories

FOR FORAGERS

Mushroom Finder fungi of North America

Ron Russo was the chief naturalist for the East Bay Regional Park District in Oakland, California.

NATURE STUDY GUIDES are published by AdventureKEEN, 2204 1st Ave. S., Suite 102, Birmingham, AL 35233; 800-678-7006; naturestudy.com. See shop.adventurewithkeen.com for our full line of nature and outdoor activity guides by ADVENTURE PUBLICATIONS, MENASHA RIDGE PRESS, and WILDERNESS PRESS, including many guides for birding, wildflowers, rocks, and trees, plus regional and national parks, hiking, camping, backpacking, and more.